# UNSUNG HEROES OF
# SOCIAL JUSTICE

by Todd Kortemeier

www.12StoryLibrary.com

12-Story Library is an imprint of Peterson Publishing Company and Press Room Editions.

Produced for 12-Story Library by Red Line Editorial

Photographs ©: New York World-Telegram and the Sun Newspaper Photograph Collection/ Library of Congress, cover, 1, 26; Dorothea Lange/FSA/OWI Collection/Library of Congress, 4; Bill Peters/The Denver Post/Getty Images, 5; Jack Harris/AP Images, 7; John Duricka/ AP Images, 8; Barry Thumma/AP Images, 9; Bettmann/Corbis, 10, 14; Owen Franken/ Corbis, 11; Julie Jacobson/AP Images, 12; Neftal/Shutterstock, 13; FSA/OWI Collection/ Library of Congress, 15; Records of the Department of Veterans Affairs, 16, 17, 28; Library of Congress, 19; Ansel Adams/Library of Congress, 20; Gary Fong/San Francisco Chronicle/ Corbis, 21; Ana Venegas/ZumaPress/Newscom, 23; Bain News Service/George Grantham Bain Collection/Library of Congress, 24, 29; George Grantham Bain Collection/Library of Congress, 25; Warren K. Leffler/U.S. News & World Report Magazine Photograph Collection/ Library of Congress, 27

**Library of Congress Cataloging-in-Publication Data**
Cataloging-in-publication information is on file with the Library of Congress.
978-1-63235-310-8 (hardcover)
978-1-63235-360-3 (paperback)
978-1-62143-474-0 (hosted ebook)

Printed in the United States of America
Mankato, MN
May, 2016

Access free, up-to-date content on this topic plus a full digital version of this book. Scan the QR code on page 31 or use your school's login at 12StoryLibrary.com.

# Table of Contents

# Lupe Anguiano Helps the Poor Find Jobs

Lupe Anguiano knew the struggles of Mexican workers well. Growing up in the 1930s, her family faced those struggles firsthand. Each May, they left their home in Colorado for California. They worked the crops there, picking fruits and vegetables. In December, they returned to Colorado. It was hard work, and it meant Anguiano missed a lot of school. But she still managed to graduate from high school.

In 1949, when she was 20 years old, Anguiano became a nun in the Roman Catholic Church. As a nun, she wanted to help the poor. Poor people and minorities faced many problems. One big problem in 1963 was racial discrimination in housing. Anguiano fought hard against laws that would make it easier for landlords to discriminate. But at the time, nuns were not supposed to be social activists. She continued her work even though church leadership told her to stop.

In 1964, Anguiano decided to leave the church and give up her work as a

A migrant family on the road in California

# $5

**Amount per week on which Anguiano lived while organizing protests around the country.**

- Anguiano originally wanted to be a nun.
- Anguiano left the church and traveled the country helping workers.
- She worked for three presidents, furthering the rights of women, Latinos, and the poor.

Anguiano advocated for minorities and people living in poverty.

nun. She traveled the country trying to help however she could. Wherever she went, she saw people living in poverty. Some needed government assistance to get by. It was hard for them to get jobs. She worked on programs that would help these people find work.

These programs led to Anguiano working for President Lyndon B. Johnson's administration. In 1965, she started working as an education specialist for the Department of Health, Education, and Welfare. Welfare is a government program that provides money to people living in poverty.

Anguiano also worked under President Richard Nixon and President Ronald Reagan. She pushed for changes in welfare, so that people could get help finding jobs, rather than just a check. In 1996, Congress passed a bill that used many of her ideas. It reformed welfare programs so that people could support their families through employment.

Anguiano also helped blaze a trail for other women and Latinos to get involved in politics. She acted as a mentor to future activists.

# Ella Baker Works Behind the Scenes for Civil Rights

The civil rights movement of the 1950s and 1960s had many great leaders. Icons, such as Martin Luther King, Jr., gave their all to earn equal rights for black people. King was the face and voice of the movement. But without Ella Baker, he might never have gotten involved. It was Baker who helped recruit King. But Baker was also a great leader. She just worked behind the scenes.

Baker grew up listening to her grandmother's stories about slavery. They were tales of slave revolts and whippings. Baker was always aware of the struggles black people faced. From an early age, she fought against injustice. Even as a college student, she protested unfair school

## BAKER'S OTHER CAUSES

Baker did not only believe in social justice for Americans. Later in life, she protested racial segregation in South Africa. She also supported independence for Puerto Rico and women's liberation around the world.

## 26
### Years Baker was actively working for social justice.

- Baker was interested in social justice as a girl.
- She moved to New York City after college and began her advocacy career.
- Baker organized the SCLC and recruited Martin Luther King, Jr.
- She worked behind the scenes organizing people and moving civil rights forward.

Baker speaks at a news conference in 1968.

## THINK ABOUT IT

Baker was a leader by setting a good example for others to follow. What do you think makes a good leader? What kind of leader are you?

the Southern Christian Leadership Conference (SCLC). It became an important advocacy group. King was its first president.

But Baker and King did not get along. Baker felt King was not inclusive of others in the movement. She believed the movement belonged to everybody, not one leader. That spoke to her leadership style. She believed in setting an example for others in line with the goals of the movement. She thought that if everyone followed her example, they would be stronger together. Baker never got the headlines herself. But she made a lot of them possible.

policies. She graduated from college at the top of her class in 1927. She then moved to New York City.

Baker got involved in several activist groups. She gained experience organizing people to protest. While in New York, she worked to end segregation in schools. In 1957, Baker moved to Atlanta. The civil rights movement was gaining strength in the South. She organized

# Frank Bowe Works to Help Americans with Disabilities

Frank Bowe lived almost his entire life without his hearing. He lost it at the age of three. But he went to college and later earned his PhD. He became an activist for the rights of people with disabilities. Bowe wanted them to have as equal a chance to succeed as anybody else.

In the 1960s and 1970s, the civil rights movement was in full swing. Women and minorities were fighting for equal rights. People with disabilities were also working for recognition. Bowe got involved in the movement in the early 1970s. In 1973, Congress passed Section 504 of the Rehabilitation Act. It guaranteed that people with disabilities would be free from discrimination. Unfortunately, this law was rarely followed.

In 1975, Bowe founded the American Coalition of Citizens with Disabilities. In early 1977, he wrote a letter to President Jimmy Carter. He asked the president to enforce the law. Nothing happened.

President Carter speaks at the White House Conference on Handicapped Individuals in 1977. Bowe wrote a letter to Carter that year asking him to enforce Section 504.

# 26

**Number of days Bowe and other activists occupied government offices in 1977.**

- Bowe lost his hearing at the age of three.
- He became an advocate for people with disabilities and started the American Coalition of Citizens with Disabilities in 1975.
- In 1977, Bowe staged nationwide sit-ins to protest the discrimination of people with disabilities.
- In 1996, he helped write a law to increase access to the Internet for people with disabilities.

President Bush signed the Americans with Disabilities Act in 1990.

So Bowe took action. He led a 10-city protest to make the government enforce Section 504. Bowe and other activists staged sit-ins. They occupied government offices around the country. By June, the law was being enforced.

Bowe went on to a career in teaching. He also advised businesses. He showed them how to make their products usable for people with disabilities. And he continued to work with the government on equal rights. In 1990, Congress passed the Americans with Disabilities Act (ADA). It was a wide-ranging set of reforms that expanded Section 504. In 1996, Bowe worked on a new law. It improved on the ADA. It helped people with disabilities use the Internet more easily.

Bowe passed away in 2007 at the age of 60. He had remained an activist late into his life. In 2006, he published a study showing that people with disabilities still faced many problems. Unemployment and poverty were issues that still needed to be addressed.

# Jacqueline Ceballos Fights for Women's Liberation

As a little girl in Louisiana in the 1930s, Jacqueline Ceballos didn't understand why there were different rules for different people. Her family, along with the rest of society, told her that a woman's place was in the home. There were few jobs that women could get. Instead, women were expected to marry and

Members of NOW protested in front of the White House. Ceballos participated in many protests and demonstrations.

have children. Ceballos challenged these ideas, even as a teenager. After college, she moved to New York, where her sister lived.

New York in the 1940s was very different from Louisiana. Ceballos was able to mix with all different kinds of people. She met women who wanted a career, not just a husband. These experiences formed her activism. She got involved with the National Organization for Women (NOW) in the late 1960s. NOW was

REVISE SOCIAL SECURITY LAWS N.O.W.

PASS the EQUAL RIGHTS AMENDMENT N.O.W.

REPEAL ABORTION LAWS N.O.W.

Best kept secret since 1923... THE EQUAL RIGHTS AMENDMENT N.O.W. demands passage this year!

The crowd at the 1972 Democratic National Convention, where Ceballos represented NOW

an activist group dedicated to ending discrimination against women.

Ceballos organized demonstrations. She started the first feminist theater. She spoke on the radio and on television. In 1970, she helped fellow feminist Betty Friedan organize the Strike for Equality. The women of NOW hung a banner on the Statue of Liberty that said, "Women of the World Unite." She was an activist for many years. She even represented NOW at the Democratic National Convention in 1972.

In 1993, Ceballos founded the Veteran Feminists of America organization. It was a group intended to honor those who fought for the women's rights movement. It helps ensure future generations know who worked for women's rights.

## 50,000
**Approximate number of women who marched down New York's Fifth Avenue during the Strike for Equality.**

- Ceballos grew up in the South, where black people and women were discriminated against.
- She moved to New York and got close to the women's movement.
- In the 1960s, Ceballos joined NOW and organized protests.
- In 1993, she founded the Veteran Feminists of America, which honors people who fought for women's rights.

# Claudette Colvin Takes a Stand by Staying Seated

The stories read pretty much the same. A young black woman gets on a bus in Montgomery, Alabama. She sits down in one of the seats reserved for white people. As the bus fills up, a white person wants her seat. But she does not move. This was the story of Rosa Parks. But it is also the story of Claudette Colvin, nine months earlier.

It was March 2, 1955. Fifteen-year-old Colvin was seated with two friends on the bus. When it came time to give up their seats so that white people could sit there, Colvin's friends moved to the back of the bus. But Colvin didn't. She refused. The bus driver called the police. Colvin was arrested and taken to jail. Colvin wasn't the first person to make a stand. Other black people had refused to give up their seats on a bus before. But Colvin was the first one who wanted to fight the bus segregation law.

Leaders of the civil rights movement had wanted to fight bus segregation for a while. Colvin's case could have been filed as a civil rights lawsuit. But some leaders felt that at 15 years old, Colvin was too young. Instead, Parks became the "face" of the Montgomery bus boycott when she refused to give up her seat in December 1955.

Colvin was not widely recognized for her contribution to the civil rights movement until later in life.

But Colvin still played a role in the desegregation of Montgomery buses. She was a key witness in the court case that overturned the law. *Browder v. Gayle* found that seating separated by race was unconstitutional. From then on, any person could sit in any open seat.

Colvin later wished that she had played a more public role. But she was proud of the role she did play. Her small action spread into a history-changing movement.

Rosa Parks is celebrated for her work on the Montgomery bus boycott.

# 42

**Age of Rosa Parks at the time she refused to give up her seat, which civil rights leaders felt made her a better symbol of the movement.**

- On March 2, 1955, 15-year-old Colvin refused to give up her seat on a bus to a white person.
- Nine months later, Rosa Parks became much more famous for the same action.
- Colvin testified in a landmark court case that made bus segregation illegal.

## THE NASHVILLE STREETCAR BOYCOTT

The Montgomery bus boycott was a landmark event in ending racial segregation. But 50 years before that, black people in Nashville, Tennessee, boycotted the city's streetcar system. And that protest also had a first hero. Mrs. W. B. Phillips refused to give up her streetcar seat. The boycott ultimately failed, but it was the first of many protests against racial segregation.

13

# Charles Hamilton Houston Defeats Jim Crow

In 1895, the United States Supreme Court ruled in a case called *Plessy v. Ferguson*. The case was about whether black people could be forced to sit in separate railroad cars from white people. The court ruled that it was okay to enforce this separation. This type of law came to be known as "separate but equal." Laws like this were called Jim Crow laws.

Also in 1895, Charles Hamilton Houston was born. He was black and from a wealthy family. Because of his family's wealth, he had more opportunities available to him than many other black people. But racism was always present. He attended college as the only black student in his class. He got good grades, but he had very few friends. When World War I broke out, Houston went to fight.

Even while fighting for his country, Houston was subject to racism. This experience helped him decide what to do with his life. Once he got back from the war, he would become a lawyer. He wanted to fight for those who could not fight back.

Houston went to Harvard Law School. As a lawyer,

Houston used his career as a lawyer to fight for civil rights.

# 200,000 to 1

**Ratio of white lawyers to black lawyers in some southern states in 1927.**

- Houston's experience with racial discrimination inspired him to become a lawyer.
- As a lawyer, he was involved in many civil rights cases that went before the Supreme Court.
- His work contributed to the overturning of all Jim Crow laws in the South, but only after his death.

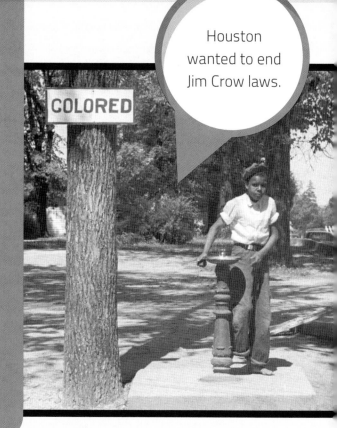

COLORED

Houston wanted to end Jim Crow laws.

Houston made it his mission to end the Jim Crow laws. He believed that could be done by winning many small cases. By building up victories over discrimination, the Supreme Court could make it illegal everywhere.

Houston focused on cases showing that "separate but equal" was not being followed. For example, in *Gaines v. Canada*, black people were not allowed to attend the state law school of Missouri. But no law school for black people existed.

There was no "equal." The court agreed with Houston.

Houston did not live to see segregation overturned in court. That would happen with the case *Brown v. Board of Education of Topeka* in 1954. Houston passed away in 1950. But his efforts were some of the first stepping stones toward desegregation.

# Callie House Works to Help Former Slaves

The victory by the North in the Civil War in 1865 made slavery illegal. But life for formerly enslaved people was still a struggle. Most of them lived in poverty. They often had no property. Callie House grew up in this era. She was born into slavery, but the war ended a few years later. House would work hard to advocate for former slaves.

In 1883, House got married. She and her husband went on to have five children. In the 1890s, she and her family moved to Nashville, Tennessee. In the state's capital, change was coming. People were talking about helping former slaves. They were talking about reparations. The idea was to provide money to former slaves so they could start a new life.

House was inspired by this idea. She helped start an organization called the National Ex-Slave Mutual Relief, Bounty and Pension Association. It was designed to make reparations a reality. She traveled all over the South to get people interested. She pushed for services and aid in the short term. But full reparations were the ultimate goal. Local chapters of her organization provided people with medical care and other aid. House sent people to Washington to ask Congress for support.

Callie House wanted to help former slaves.

A certificate of membership in the Ex-Slave Mutual Relief, Bounty and Pension Association

House's movement was not popular with white southern people. Some black leaders did not approve either. They didn't want to waste time with ideas that they felt had no chance of ever happening. House was accused of misleading black people.

In 1916, House was formally accused of tricking people into donating money to a hopeless cause. An all-white, all-male jury convicted her of this crime. House served almost a year in jail. When she got out, she returned to her life before activism. She worked doing laundry. But her success in organizing people is something that would influence the civil rights movement decades later.

# 300,000
**Number of members House's organization had in 1900.**

- House grew up after slavery had ended.
- She heard about the reparations movement and decided to get involved.
- She pushed for services and aid for former slaves.

# Helen Hunt Jackson Sees the Struggles of American Indians

For Helen Hunt Jackson, writing started as a way to deal with sadness. By the time she was 30 in 1860, she had lost her parents, her husband, and both her sons. Writing was a way to handle it all. But it became more than that. She used it to call attention to a big injustice.

## 300

**Number of printings of Jackson's novel *Ramona*.**

- Jackson started writing to deal with personal loss.
- After seeing a speech by Chief Standing Bear, she wrote about injustice faced by American Indians.
- Her novel *Ramona*, about American Indians in California, introduced more people to the struggles of American Indians.

Jackson was born in Massachusetts. But she suffered from poor health. Her doctor recommended she move to Colorado, where the air was cleaner. In Colorado Springs, she met and married her second husband, William. She published poetry collections, travel books, and books for children. She sometimes wrote using a man's name, because women often had a harder time getting published.

In 1879, on a trip back east, Jackson saw a speech by Chief Standing Bear. He was speaking

## THE REAL RAMONA

*Ramona* is considered one of the greatest books written about California. It remained popular and has been made into plays and films. The ultimate honor came in 1894, when the town of Nuevo, California, was renamed Ramona.

Jackson became famous for her novel about the struggles of American Indians.

Jackson published several essays on the subject. But it was a novel that got the most attention. *Ramona* was published in 1884. It was about the struggles of American Indians in California. Reviews were positive. But people liked the book more than its message. Jackson was disappointed.

at an event about the struggles of American Indians. Jackson learned that many American Indians had been displaced from their land. She decided to bring attention to this issue through her writing. But she knew that because she was a woman, it would be hard to get people to listen.

Jackson died less than a year after *Ramona* came out. While it had not been what she intended, she had created a beloved book. And it introduced the struggles of American Indians to a wide audience.

19

# Fred Korematsu Defies Japanese-American Internment

Japan's attack on the US Navy base at Pearl Harbor in 1941 surprised many Americans. It was a scary time. The US government became suspicious of anyone with Japanese heritage. It worried that these people were loyal to Japan and would spy for the enemy. Even people born in the United States to Japanese parents were not trusted. They had not committed any crimes. But the US government relocated 120,000 of them to internment camps around the western United States.

Fred Korematsu was supposed to be relocated. His parents came to the United States from Japan in 1905. They settled in Oakland, California. Korematsu was born there. As a boy,

## $20,000

**Amount awarded by the US government in 1998 to any living person who had spent time in an internment camp.**

- After the Japanese bombed Pearl Harbor in 1941, the US government rounded up Japanese Americans into camps.
- Korematsu refused to go and was arrested.
- He appealed his case to the Supreme Court, but lost.
- Korematsu was retried and found innocent in 1981.

An internment camp in California

he loved playing American sports, such as baseball. A teacher first called him Fred because his real Japanese name was hard to say. But he liked Fred so much he used it for the rest of his life. Korematsu considered himself a loyal American. Korematsu even tried to sign up for the US military. But he was told that Japanese Americans were not allowed.

In February 1942, President Franklin Roosevelt ordered that Japanese Americans be sent to camps. Korematsu was 23 years old. His parents went, but he refused. He ran. He even had surgery to make his eyes look more Caucasian. But in May 1942, he was caught. He was accused of being a spy.

Korematsu decided to fight. He knew this policy was wrong. Korematsu was freed from jail but was sent to an internment camp. His case ended up going all the way to the Supreme Court. But he lost. The court ruled that the government had the right to intern its own citizens.

Korematsu was embarrassed he had lost. He felt responsible for allowing the internment to happen. And he was not a hero to other Japanese Americans. Many Japanese Americans had gone along with internment to prove their loyalty to the United States. Many felt Korematsu was just a troublemaker.

Justice did not come until 1981. A historian asked the government to look at the case again. Korematsu, who was 64 years old by that time, was found innocent. Never again could Americans be interned just because of their ethnicity.

Later in life, Korematsu was found innocent of being a spy.

# Felicitas Mendez Helps End Segregation in California

Racial segregation in schools did not happen only in the southern United States. In the 1940s, it was common in southern California. There, it applied mainly to the separation of Mexican Americans from white Americans. And it wasn't just schools. Theaters, parks, and restaurants were the same way.

Sylvia Mendez was one child who attended a non-white school. Most of the other students there came from poor families. Their parents typically worked in farm fields. Sylvia's parents were better off than most. Felicitas and Gonzalo Mendez owned their farm. Some of Sylvia's cousins went to the white school, only because they had lighter-colored skin.

The Mendezes were upset. They were American citizens. Why should there be different schools for different races? They decided to fight it. The school offered to let Sylvia in. But the Mendezes said no. They demanded that all Hispanic children be let in.

## 5,000
**Approximate number of Mexican-American children affected by the Mendez case.**

- Schools in the 1940s were segregated by race.
- In southern California, there were separate schools for white children and schools for Mexican Americans.
- The Mendez family filed a lawsuit to integrate the schools.
- They won, and this case was a starting point to desegregate schools in the United States.

While Gonzalo spent his days working on the case, Felicitas ran the farm. Without a steady income, there would be no way to pay the lawyers. With Felicitas running things, the farm became even more successful. She also organized other families to take part in the case. The Mendezes were able to pay for lawyers for themselves and other families.

When the case went to trial in 1947, the judge ruled there was no reason to segregate the schools. They found the non-white students were not getting an equal-quality education. In 1954, the Mendez case would be used in an even bigger case. *Brown v. Board of Education of Topeka* overturned all school segregation in the United States.

The Mendezes returned to normal life. Gonzalo passed away in 1964, and Felicitas died in 1998. Now there are several schools named for them in southern California.

The Mendez children pose by a photograph of their parents, Felicitas and Gonzalo.

# Inez Milholland Works Tirelessly for Women's Rights

Today, Inez Milholland is less known than other members of the women's rights movement. But in her time, she was one of the most visible. She used costumes and powerful symbols to make people notice the struggles of women everywhere.

Milholland was born in 1886. As a child, she spent time in both New York and London. Her family was wealthy, and she got a good education. But even the all-female Vassar College she attended did not support the women's rights movement. Milholland was not allowed to organize protests at Vassar. So she organized events off campus instead. This was the start of her leadership role in the women's suffrage movement.

In 1913, she helped organize her biggest event. She led a parade of women marching on Washington, DC. She rode a white horse and wore a long white cape. The parade was meant to bring attention to getting women the right to vote. It took place the day before President Woodrow Wilson was sworn in.

Milholland led a parade to support women's suffrage.

Milholland continued traveling the country advocating for the vote. But she had other causes as well. She was against the death penalty. She had also a law degree. She tried to reform police and the courts to make them more fair.

Milholland suffered from poor health. She had a condition that caused her to become easily weak and tired. Her constant travel did not help. She collapsed during a 1916 speech and died ten weeks later. She was only 30 years old. She did not live to see women get the vote in 1920. But her work helped make it happen.

Milholland was also against the death penalty and wanted to make courts more fair.

## 5,000
**Approximate number of women Milholland led in the 1913 Washington, DC parade.**

- Milholland was born to a wealthy family and received a top education.
- At Vassar College, she was not allowed to organize protests.
- Milholland led a parade for women's voting rights in 1913.
- She died in 1916, four years before women got the right to vote.

## MILHOLLAND'S ANTI-WAR ACTIVISM

In 1915, Milholland went to Europe as a journalist covering World War I. She was against the war and wrote from that perspective. While working in Italy, she was kicked out of the country for her antiwar views.

25

# Bayard Rustin Organizes the March on Washington

The 1963 March on Washington became one of the greatest moments of the civil rights movement. There had never been a protest like it before. The man at the heart of it was Bayard Rustin. His job was to organize the march.

Rustin was an unlikely person for the job. He did have a long history of working for civil rights. But he was also gay and a socialist. Those were both dangerous things to be in the 1960s. So Rustin kept these things secret. The march was to be the biggest demonstration ever. He didn't want anything to get in the way.

One of Rustin's biggest goals was making the march nonviolent. That was something that came from his religious background. Before Rustin, civil rights leaders had been

Rustin was an activist for the civil rights movement.

Rustin spoke at a press conference for the March on Washington.

next year. The act formally outlawed discrimination based on race or gender.

Rustin continued to work to advance the rights of black people. Near the end of his life, he came out publicly as a gay man. He worked to raise awareness of AIDS in the 1980s. Rustin died in 1987. Fifty years after the march, his contributions to civil rights were recognized. In 2013, he was awarded the Presidential Medal of Freedom.

prepared to use violence in their protests. Rustin convinced them that their cause would be better understood with peace.

The march turned out to be a massive success. It was where Dr. Martin Luther King, Jr., gave his famous "I Have a Dream" speech. Because of the nonviolent approach, there were only four arrests. The Civil Rights Act was passed the

## 200,000
**Approximate number of protesters at the 1963 March on Washington.**

- Rustin was a civil rights leader.
- His life as a gay man and socialist made him stay behind the scenes.
- Rustin is best remembered for organizing the 1963 March on Washington.
- He worked later in life for gay rights.

## THINK ABOUT IT

Rustin hid important details of his life so that people would take him seriously. Do you think this was the right thing to do? Why or why not?

27

# Fact Sheet

- In the 1800s, the United States expanded westward. Many American Indian populations were forcibly moved off their homelands during this time. Many people died during this process. More than 100,000 American Indians were moved starting in 1830.

- Women in the United States actively sought the right to vote beginning in the 1820s. Some states began to grant women the right in the early 20th century. But it was not until 1920 that all women got the right to vote with the passage of the 19th Amendment.

- The civil rights movement in the United States took place nearly 100 years after slavery ended. Black people still faced discrimination. In 1954, laws separating schools by race were overturned. Protests continued throughout the 1950s and 1960s. The Civil Rights Act of 1964 ended all legal discrimination by race.

- The Montgomery bus boycott took place in Montgomery, Alabama. It lasted from December 5, 1955, to December 20, 1956. To protest the discriminatory seating policies on the buses, people refused to ride buses in Montgomery. Segregated seating was eventually eliminated and the boycott ended.

- During the civil rights movement, women in the United States began arguing for fair treatment. Women faced discrimination in employment and education. The Civil Rights Act of 1964 addressed this by making gender discrimination illegal.

- The Americans with Disabilities Act (ADA) was passed in 1990. It makes sure people with disabilities are not discriminated against. It provides equal opportunities for people with disabilities, such as accessible bathrooms and access to transportation. It was updated in 2010. The update set new standards for constructing accessible buildings, among other updates.

# Glossary

**activist**
A person who takes action to promote a cause about which he or she feels strongly.

**advocacy**
The act of fighting for a particular cause.

**Congress**
Term for the United States House of Representatives and Senate.

**feminist**
A person who believes that women's rights and opportunities should be equal to men's.

**internment**
The forcing of people into a confined area.

**journalist**
A person who writes and reports on news stories.

**jury**
A collection of people put together during a trial to decide if a person is guilty or innocent.

**nun**
A woman who takes a vow to devote her life to a specific religion.

**segregation**
The practice of separating places, such as schools or restaurants, according to race.

**sit-in**
A type of protest in which people occupy a place by staying there for a long time.

**socialist**
A person who believes in socialism, a political theory that believes the community should control and own the production and distribution of products and services.

# For More Information

## Books

Beckner, Chrisanne. *100 African-Americans Who Shaped American History*. Milwaukee, WI: World Almanac Library, 2015.

Nagara, Innosanto. *A Is for Activist*. New York: Seven Stories Press, 2013.

Ross, Michael Elsohn. *She Takes a Stand: 16 Fearless Activists Who Have Changed the World*. Chicago: Chicago Review Press, 2015.

## Visit 12StoryLibrary.com

Scan the code or use your school's login at **12StoryLibrary.com** for recent updates about this topic and a full digital version of this book. Enjoy free access to:

- Digital ebook
- Breaking news updates
- Live content feeds
- Videos, interactive maps, and graphics
- Additional web resources

**Note to educators:** Visit 12StoryLibrary.com/register to sign up for free premium website access. Enjoy live content plus a full digital version of every 12-Story Library book you own for every student at your school.

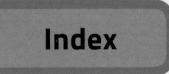

# Index

## About the Author

Todd Kortemeier is a writer from Minneapolis, Minnesota. He is a graduate of the University of Minnesota's School of Journalism & Mass Communication. He has authored many books for young people.

## READ MORE FROM 12-STORY LIBRARY

Every 12-Story Library book is available in many formats. For more information, visit 12StoryLibrary.com.